AROUND
BISHOP'S CLEEVE
AND
WINCHCOMBE
IN OLD PHOTOGRAPHS

A FASCINATING PICTURE of The George Inn at Winchcombe c. 1870. Stephen's coach from Broadway stopped there at 9.30 a.m. every Tuesday, Thursday and Saturday on its way to Cheltenham. The present front of The George is a late Victorian reconstruction.

Front cover illustration.
THIS PHOTOGRAPH symbolises the links between *Bishop's Cleeve to Winchcombe in Old Photographs* and this book. The Kitchen brothers were also on the cover of that book. Here they are accompanied by their neice, Miss Smith. The date and place: c. 1915 at Upper Breeches, Nottingham Hill, are the same.

AROUND
BISHOP'S CLEEVE
AND
WINCHCOMBE
IN OLD PHOTOGRAPHS

COLLECTED BY

DAVID H. ALDRED

Budding
BOOKS

A Budding Book

First published in 1989 by Alan Sutton Publishing Limited

This edition published in 2000 by Budding Books,
an imprint of Sutton Publishing Limited
Phoenix Mill · Thrupp · Stroud · Gloucestershire GL5 2BU

A catalogue record for this book is available from the British Library

ISBN 1-84015-151-X

This book is dedicated to Tim Curr and John Doxsey without whose generosity
neither of my two collections of photographs would have been possible.

Typesetting and origination by
Sutton Publishing Limited.
Printed in Great Britain by
Redwood Books, Trowbridge, Wiltshire

CONTENTS

INTRODUCTION

No sooner had *Bishop's Cleeve to Winchcombe in Old Photographs* appeared two years ago, than I was inundated with offers of more old photographs of the area. This volume is the result, but it would not have appeared without the generosity of the many people I acknowledge at the end of the collection.

One of the pleasures gained from compiling this new volume is that it has given me the opportunity to follow up some of the themes and questions of the earlier collection and I hope readers will use the two books side by side. Some photographs give further glimpses into scenes and events portrayed in that first volume – Winchcombe carnival, work on the farm in Gretton, post-war development in Woodmancote. Others help to complement earlier scenes by showing change over time – Reverend C.D. Walker, pictured as the curate at Winchcombe, can be seen here as rector of Woolstone; we can trace Abbey Terrace's development from open space to car park. Further photographs have allowed me to fill in some of the gaps noted in the earlier collection – Sudeley prisoners of war, Old Farm in Bishop's Cleeve as a tea garden, and some traditional farming scenes. I am also able to record an answer to one of the questions I posed then – where were Southam Fields and who were photographed there (p. 151)? The scene was photographed near Meadoway in Bishop's Cleeve (not Southam!) and the central figure with straw hat and pitchfork was Henry Wiltshire. He bought two fields in 1912–13 and the photograph probably commemorated his first harvest. My thanks go to John Parker of Sheepscombe, Henry Wiltshire's grandson, for this information. Many other people have given me names of individuals I did not know, or corrected inaccuracies in the captions. To them, also, I owe thanks. I have attempted to cover a larger area than in the first volume, principally because I was offered photographs from farther afield. As a result this collection covers an area starting in Prestbury, which has enabled me to use Betty Mustoe's wonderful collection of race photographs, and extends to Laverton and Buckland, which has enabled me to use Lord Neidpath's collection of calotypes. (Calotypes were an early form of photograph, relying on paper negatives and exposures of up to two minutes – consequently landscapes were preferred to portraits.)

The book itself, however, remains a series of snapshots in time rather than a complete history of the area for there are many gaps, in time as well as more obviously in place, but I have only been able to include photographs made available to me. Nevertheless the area covered does allow us to make some observations on life over the last 130 years, and trace the way in which a rural area has been influenced by change. In 1860, the date of the earliest photographs included here, only Prestbury showed signs of 'modernisation' as Cheltenham spread its influences. Today, electricity, mains water and television are almost universal throughout the area and only on its fringes, particularly at Stanway, does the village still look much as it did in 1860, although the outward appearance masks the inner changes. As noted later in the volume, Stanton provides an interesting example of Sir Philip Stott trying to increase the 'traditional' face of the village after he bought it in 1906.

Yet change did not affect all communities at the same time: Cleeve Hill experienced its main development before the First World War; Bishop's Cleeve after the arrival of Smith's industries in 1939; Winchcombe with the mass ownership of the motor car in the 1960s; while places like Alderton, Gretton, Teddington and Toddington were affected rather later, in the 1970s. However, subtle change can occur in any period as the writers of the small number of books written about the area in the period under study were able to detect. I have included two photographs from Henry Branch's book *Cotswold and Vale*, written in 1904. This is what he wrote about Winchcombe:

> The dwellers in the great cities would find balm and repose in Cheltenham; the Cheltonian enjoys, for a change, the quietude of Winchcombe; and Winchcombe in its turn thinks itself high pressure by contrast with Sudeley, or Gretton, or Stanway, or Stanley Pontlarge or Charlton Abbots, or the other villages round about.

Fifteen years later Dr John Henry Garrett in his book *From A Cotswold Height* (now reprinted as an Alan Sutton paperback) wrote of Bishop's Cleeve:

> But a greater modernity, due to touch with the fashionable town that lies but three miles away, shows its influence on sons and daughters who have lived there and have returned, or who go to and fro daily by bicycle or train, bringing back with them innovations of dress and ideas, manners and speech.

For a detailed description of farmlife during the years of transition from traditional agriculture to today's highly mechanised industry, I recommend readers to dip into *The Family Farmer* by F.D. Smith and Barbara Wilcox, describing life on Bengrove Farm around the time of the last war.

In the writing of any book there comes a time to call 'stop'. In doing so I am conscious of the shortcomings of this collection: gaps in the coverage of the area; unnamed faces in group photographs, which with time might be corrected. However, I trust the photographs here will be a means to remind readers, residents and visitors alike, of 'the day before yesterday'. I have divided them into the sections which seem to make the greatest sense. I start with a general survey of the area, taking the theme of change, before moving on to people at leisure, then people who seem to be doing nothing except deliberately posing for the camera. Where possible and appropriate, I have tried to add names to increase the enjoyment of friends and relatives. From people we move to buildings and some of the oldest photographs in the book, then to a section showing the variety of ways in which people have earned a living in the area, before considering transport and the wider world. Obviously some photographs fall under more than one heading, but I trust my choices make sense and link the individual photographs by some common threads which will increase the reader's enjoyment in rediscovering some of the vanished scenes from this beautiful part of the country.

WOOD STANWAY C.1870. Note the seemingly poor condition of the house on the left, and the washing drying on the fence.

Changed Scenes

IN THIS SECTION the photographs are arranged to lead from the outskirts of Cheltenham to Laverton and Buckland. This view of Prestbury dates from c. 1930 and shows the tram tracks. The timber-framed cottage on the right was demolished for road widening 30 years ago.

MILL STREET, Prestbury, in 1958. The scene is still recognizable today, showing that, even in Prestbury, change has not obliterated all traces of the past.

CHURCH ROAD, Bishop's Cleeve, at the end of the last century. Here change is more obvious. Note the yoke and pails. A village pump lay beyond the houses on the right.

A PRE-WAR GLIMPSE of the next stretch of Church Road. Two Salvation Army missioners are watched by three boys and a dog.

THE MESSAGE ON THIS FRITH POSTCARD describes the village as 'lovely and restful'. The remarkable fact is that it was written in August 1957 when many people would have considered the village already spoiled by recent development.

A GENERAL VIEW before post-war expansion, showing the village surrounded by fields.

THE PRIORY has changed little since 1965, but the fields beyond are now built upon.

THIS SCENE is unrecognizable today. Bert Long's cows graze in fields where Ashfield and Oakfield Roads now lie. Fieldgate House, however, provides a landmark for reference.

A RARE PHOTOGRAPH capturing the great changes in Bishop's Cleeve actually in progress. Only part of Minett's Avenue had been built by February 1954 when this scene was captured.

BISHOP'S CLEEVE is now joined to Woodmancote. This view of 1968 shows just how much Station Road has changed in the last 20 years.

HERE IS ANOTHER SHORT SEQUENCE showing development around Woodmancote Green to complement that shown in *Bishop's Cleeve to Winchcombe in Old Photographs*. Poplar Farm is clearly visible on the left in this view of c. 1954.

TEN YEARS LATER, and the Pottersfield development begins. . . .

... AND THE FIRST HOUSES rise from the ground!

ANOTHER EARLIER WOODMANCOTE THEME expanded here is the winter of 1947. Drifts outside Northam Stores at the top of Station Road.

AS DESCRIBED IN THE INTRODUCTION, Cleeve Hill had been developed by 1914 as a health resort and fashionable outer suburb of Cheltenham. A popular view taken from the common looking north.

THE TRAMWAY, reaching the Malvern View in 1901, accelerated these changes. The wagon belonged to Arthur Yiend who built many of the houses on the hill dating from this period.

Cleeve Hill, Cheltenham.

A MARVELLOUS PERIOD POSTCARD of trippers walking on the hill in the pre-First World War heyday of the resort.

THE FIRST EXAMPLE in this collection of a postcard by Butts of Bourton. It shows residential development on the slopes of the hill in the 1920s and the 'Tin Tabernacle' free church, now demolished.

ANOTHER NEIGHBOUR OF BISHOP'S CLEEVE, Gotherington, has experienced less dramatic change than Woodmancote. These two views along Malleson Road probably date from 1910–20 and the 1930s respectively.

STATION ROAD was not a familiar name for this road. Rhondda Cottage is recognizable on the right.

A VIEW of the other end of the village taken early this century.

THE DEMOLITION of the timber-framed building on the right is the only major change since this photograph was taken nearly 50 years ago.

WOOLSTONE has experienced less change than Gotherington. There could never have been a great demand for postcards, but some were published. This dates from c. 1910.

HOW MANY ENTHUSIASTS at Prescott Hill Climb would recognize this view taken shortly before the course was built in 1936?

THE FIRST OF THIS SEQUENCE of Winchcombe photographs has been chosen to show how, superficially, there has been little change in many places. Compare this scene, c. 1870, with that of today.

PERCY SIMMS of Chipping Norton produced many postcards of the area before the last war. Again, little change obviously appears to have taken place in this part of Winchcombe.

ON THIS POSTCARD, posted in May 1915, the writer describes Winchcombe as 'quiet and solitary'. This scene has not changed much even today, but the description might be different!

ONLY THE CLOTHES and distant gaslamp give a period atmosphere here, but the card was posted in August 1913.

THE CROSS was a favourite subject for postcards. Both these cards were produced by Tovey's of Winchcombe. Compare the front of The George with that shown in the frontispiece. Emma Dent 'restored' it in the mid-1880s.

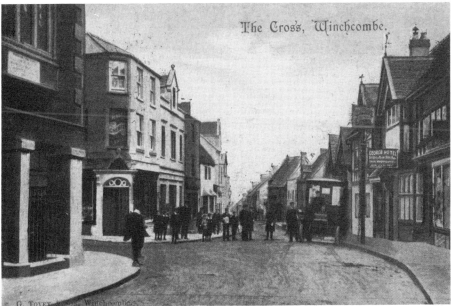

The Cross, Winchcombe.

ALTHOUGH THE ORIGINAL CARD is heavily colour tinted, it is of interest as the bus is presumably the one that ran between Winchcombe and Bishop's Cleeve from 1 February to 1 June 1905 before completion of the railway.

423. THE CROSS, WINCHCOMBE

GEORGE QUANT of Westwood House in the High Street also produced postcards of Winchcombe at that time. This card shows the importance of human and animal power before the motor age.

THE GASLAMP AND COAL WAGON give a period atmosphere to another of Tovey's postcards from the turn of the century.

INTERESTINGLY, this card shows George Quant's premises in the High Street.

NOTE THE CHANGES occuring between these two cards. Gaslamp and horse have been replaced by electric lamp and motor car. Winchcombe was first supplied with electricity in 1928.

THESE TWO SCENES are very similar to those on page 88 of *Bishop's Cleeve to Winchcombe in Old Photographs*. They show that North Street was also a popular subject for turn-of-the-century postcards. This is another of Quant's cards.

A RATHER EARLIER VIEW than that on p. 88, but Tovey's bookshop is still surrounded by news placards!

THESE TWO SIMILAR VIEWS of Abbey Terrace show its development from open space....

... TO CAR PARK. This card was posted in 1954.

ANOTHER OF TOVEY'S LOCAL SCENES. The Vicarage, built in 1845, is now a private house.

AN ILLUSTRATION from *Cotswold and Vale* mentioned in the Introduction. Interestingly the photograph was taken by Dr Garrett, the author of the other book quoted in the Introduction. The title of the picture is 'A May Day at Winchcombe'.

TO CLOSE THIS SEQUENCE OF WINCHCOMBE VIEWS, these two postcards are evidence of total change. Recent developments have changed this scene of the mill dam, taken in the 1920s, beyond all recognition.

WINCHCOMBE AND SUDELEY HILL

ALTHOUGH THE CHURCH, school buildings and neighbouring houses are instantly recognizable, the fields in the foreground have long been built upon. The writing on the back of the card described Winchcombe as 'such a quaint town' in October 1928.

THE GASWORKS were an important feature of Winchcombe from the 1850s to the 1960s. This aerial view dates from shortly before their demolition.

MOVING ON FROM WINCHCOMBE, this is Didbrook c.1860. The stones are, presumably, to be used to fill up the holes in the road.

THE RIVER ISBOURNE AT TODDINGTON MANOR; this appears timeless, but the postcard dates from the 1920s at the latest.

FURTHER FROM WINCHCOMBE change seems less apparent. The continued existence of the Stanway estate has been a powerful influence in controlling development. These two cottages on the estate were photographed c. 1860.

THIS COULD BE TODAY. It was, in fact, 1860! There is a complete absence of change – compare it with any of the photographs of the centre of Winchcombe.

WHEN SIR PHILIP STOTT bought Stanton in 1906 he actually discouraged change. He even moved three timber-framed barns into the village to increase its rustic appearance. Only the lack of tarmac and style of car betray an early twentieth century date for this photograph.

STANTON COURT (GLOS.)

THIS WARTIME VIEW of Stanton has added interest because it was sent from Stanton Court itself and signed by G.E. Stott.

THE REALITY OF THE COTSWOLDS 130 years ago contrasts strongly with the popular image portrayed in many guidebooks. This calotype taken in Laverton shows a house with cracks in the walls and a thatched roof badly in need of repair. At this time many thatched roofs were being replaced by stone slates from Stanway Hill. Note the shadowy figures in the doorway – evidence of the long exposure needed for calotypes.

ANOTHER VIEW OF LAVERTON from the same date. The buildings appear in better condition, but cracks are still apparent to the careful observer.

ARRIVING IN ALDERTON, this short sequence emphasizes the poor living conditions compared with those of today. A photograph taken c. 1905.

AT A SIMILAR DATE, note the hayricks in the farmyard. The disappearance of farms from village centres has been another change in the present century.

THE METHODIST CHAPEL, built in 1899, was quite new when this photograph was taken. It is now a private house.

THE SQUARE IN 1925. Note the Maypole.

TEDDINGTON c. 1920. The houses on the left still stand, but the orchards have since given way to houses. Bill Harris, the local scrap-dealer, passes through on his way home to Alstone.

MANY PEOPLE who regularly travel between Teddington and Alstone would not recognize this as the turning to Bengrove. These two houses, photographed c. 1920, no longer exist.

THE 'LEISURE AND PLEASURE' SECTION starts here with the first example from Betty Mustoe's extensive collection on the Cheltenham races. Outside the Weighing Room over 50 years ago.

Leisure and Pleasure

BETTY MUSTOE comes from the well-known Roberts family of race horse trainers of Prestbury. In 1954 her brother, John, trained 'Four Ten', the Gold Cup winner. At the second fence it may be seen second from the right.

THE MOMENT OF GLORY! Tommy Cusack is photographed glancing behind as he passes the post.

TRAINER JOHN ROBERTS, 'Four Ten' and jockey Tommy Cusack after the victory.

RACING OF A DIFFERENT KIND NEXT. Prescott Hill Climb in 1957, showing the course before the construction of the loop in 1962.

AT THE SAME MEETING a Bugatti takes the climb driven by Ronnie Symundson.

A VIEW OF THE PADDOCK.

ANOTHER VIEW of the paddock 30 years ago.

MOVING NOW ALONG the road to Gretton, Margaret Pullen has generously made available more photographs from her collection of Gretton festivities. Here is another view of the 'Victory' float celebrating George VI's coronation. Margaret and her sister Jesse are the sailors and her father, Frank Taylor, is Nelson.

QUEEN ELIZABETH'S CORONATION CARNIVAL of 1953. Dora Roberts and Mary Nicholas as 'Darby and Joan'.

IN THE SAME CARNIVAL came Albert Davis as a cowboy and Jim Davis pushing his grandmother in the pram!

THIS PHOTOGRAPH of the procession reminds us how comparatively unusual motor transport was in 1953.

AT A RATHER EARLIER DATE – 1926 – horse power was the usual form of transport. 'Short' pulls holiday visitors around Gretton.

LOCAL COMMUNITIES organizing their own activities has been a constant feature of rural life. This patriotic carnival took place in Winchcombe in 1907.

THE FIRST CARNIVAL had taken place the year before, 1906, in Sudeley grounds on August Bank Holiday Monday. C. Sirett, photographer and stationer, of Blockley produced the postcards.

ANOTHER VIEW of the same carnival – a real period piece!

'MERRIE ENGLANDE' revived by the Maypole dancers of 1922. This was the last year the flower show took place at Sudeley.

A FLOAT FOR WINCHCOMBE FÊTE in 1928. Jack Surman driving; Mr Beard as Father Time; Tom Gaskins with the yoke; Frank Iles in the top hat; Rocky Cotterell in the bowler.

THIS IS ACTUALLY ON CLEEVE HILL! Highbury scout troop in Cheltenham was one of the earliest troops to be founded, in 1907. This photograph was taken at its camp on Cleeve Hill the following year.

AT THE FOOT OF CLEEVE HILL, Woodmancote continues to be a lively community. Here a procession leaves The Green in the early 1950s.

THE CHAPEL SUNDAY SCHOOL held a sale in 1959 in what is now the Old Village Hall. Helpers and customers crowd the stalls.

NEITHER LEISURE NOR PLEASURE! For the last 30 years the Curr family has provided countless players for Woodmancote cricket club. In 1963 Tim and Pat help repair the square.

THE SLEDGE RUN above the cricket ground in December 1964.

A CLOSE RUN RACE at Bishop's Cleeve Secondary School's sports day 25 years ago.

'MERRIE ENGLANDE' AGAIN. Morris dancers in Church Road, Bishop's Cleeve, in 1957.

Part of Bishops Cleeve Pleasure Gdns

BISHOP'S CLEEVE TO WINCHCOMBE IN OLD PHOTOGRAPHS contained many photographs of Eversfield House tea-gadens in Station Road, Bishop's Cleeve. The homemade nature of the attractions are clearly visible in this further view – but the enjoyment was immense!

MOVING ON to more genteel activities – Reverend C.D. Walker opens the Fête at Woolstone rectory in 1934 or 1935.

A STALL at the same fête – a study in hats.

NOBODY IS QUITE SURE ABOUT THIS EVENT. It is probably in Alderton c.1910 with the Winchcombe band. It is possibly 'Club Day' – Trinity Monday when the Alderton Friendly Society organized extensive activities.

COULD THIS BE THE SAME EVENT with the band having moved into the village to continue the celebration? Note the Maypole, featured on page 40 in the previous section.

AN IMPORTANT EVENT in the life of the community in Alderton was the opening of the village hall in 1922. It has recently been extensively rebuilt.

A WHIT MONDAY FÊTE in the Old Rectory c. 1926.

THE REASONS for this group of Cosmic schoolchildren c. 1933 is not clear but older readers might remember their names. Back row, left to right: Iris Evans, Dora Hobbs, Violet ?, Molly Larner, Minnie Hobbs. Front row: Ruth Fletcher, Gwen Williams, Edith Evans.

THIS SECTION CLOSES with a further example of 'Merrie Englande'. Under the patronage of Stanway House, the English Folk Dance Society held several festivals in the grounds between the wars. These merrymakers were photographed in 1925.

Just People

SOME PHOTOGRAPHS IN THIS SECTION have been chosen because they are typical of a vanished way of life. Shepherd Curtis at Didbrook before the First World War.

THESE WORTHIES organized the Winchcombe Carnivals pictured in the previous section.

THE CLEEVE HILL BOARD OF CONSERVATORS photographed at one of their quarterly meetings, c. 1935.

ONE OF THE FASCINATIONS of volumes such as this comes from studying school photographs. This photograph of Slatter's prep school in 1916 complements the one in my earlier book. Mrs Slatter with daughter Daisy and 13 children.

THERE ARE MANY CONTRASTS between the top photograph and the other three on these two pages: size of class, clothes, general health and ease in front of a camera, but they are all Winchcombe schoolchildren.

ANOTHER CLASS at the school in Back Lane, photographed in 1914.

A PROBLEM IN PRESENTING LARGE SCHOOL GROUPS lies in finding all the names. A further problem lies in presenting all those names in the space available. It is hoped that readers will still be able to take pleasure from recognizing familiar faces in these and later photographs.

STANTON SCHOOL closed after the last war – a fate of several small Cotswold schools. Mrs Finch is the teacher.

DIDBROOK SCHOOL at the turn of the century. Unlike Stanton this school still survives.

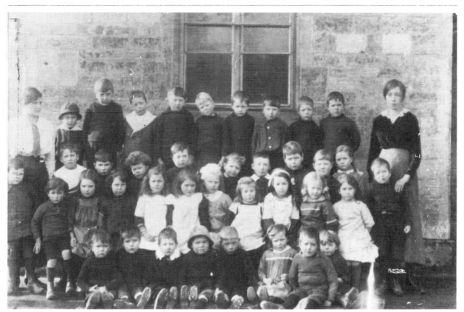

BISHOP'S CLEEVE SCHOOL can no longer be regarded as the small village school recorded here in 1917 with teachers Winnie Gaskins on the left and Winnie Surman on the right.

IT IS TOO EASY TO FORGET the importance of the Sunday School as a place of learning for many village children. The staff and scholars of Gotherington pose in front of the village chapel in 1913.

EARLY IN THE LIFE OF BISHOP'S CLEEVE SECONDARY SCHOOL many foreign visits were organized by John Crouch. He is seen at the back on the left with this party to Lausanne in 1960, accompanied by colleagues Elizabeth Elsmore and Don Luker.

CROSS COUNTRY WINNERS from the same date: R. Surman, J. Morgan, A. Peart.

REFERENCE WAS MADE on page 69 to the growth in Bishop's Cleeve primary school. In 1965 the infant school moved to new buildings. By 1968 classrooms were already crowded, as this photograph shows.

IN FINE WEATHER lessons moved outside. The Nursery Railway in 1969.

THE INFANTS had overflowed into new classrooms intended for the junior school by 1970. It had not yet moved from its traditional buildings opposite the church.

ALTHOUGH THESE PHOTOGRAPHS OF THE SCHOOL are some of the most recent in the book, these seven year-old Roman citizens are now nearly thirty!

A GROUP OF YOUNGSTERS — but not at school. Winchcombe Scouts at camp at Sudeley in 1939.

BISHOP'S CLEEVE PARISH CHURCH, May, 1931. Older readers will remember the worthies in the second row: Miss Tarling (organist), Mr Franks (churchwarden), Revd H. Morgan Brown (rector), Revd Hippesly Smith (curate), Mr Shacklock (churchwarden).

REFERENCE HAS ALREADY BEEN MADE to the Trinity Monday Club Day held by Alderton Friendly Society which offered its members financial help in sickness and death. These two photographs show scenes from 1937–8. Note the proudly displayed banners in front of the village hall.

IN FRONT OF THE GALLOPING HORSES on the village green, probably in the same year.

A FEATURE OF THE CLUB DAYS was the playing of the village band, photographed here c. 1938. The last Club Day was held in 1940.

NOT CLUB DAY, but helpers at the 1937 Coronation celebrations.

MORE HELPERS on this page, but at Stanway.

THESE TWO PHOTOGRAPHS are useful reminders of the importance of Stanway House for the local area throughout the years covered by this book – an influence which still exists today.

WE NOW MOVE TO A SEQUENCE OF SPORTS PHOTOGRAPHS. Winchcombe Bowling Club played near the old swimming pool on the River Isbourne. Their green was destroyed to grow vegetables during the last war.

ALDERTON FOOTBALL TEAM, 1926–27.

REFERENCE HAS ALREADY BEEN MADE to Woodmancote Cricket Club on page 56. This was their team in 1933.

AND THIS IS THE TEAM for whom the square was rebuilt. Back row: J. Williams, O. Dungey, D. Hatton, D. Goring, D. Curr. Centre row: C. Rogers, L. Williamson, P. Curr, C. Smith. Front row: A. Larner, T. N. Curr, M. Worgan.

WOODMANCOTE FOOTBALL TEAM at the time of the First World War c.1916. Their names are all known: Back row, left to right: T. Jeanes, C. Hatton, H. Draper, F. Jones, B. Gilder, W. Roberts, G. Coombes, H. Smith, R. Agg, F. Ballinger, F. Eustace, J. Gilder, T. Eustace, E. Wasley, R. Surman. Front row, left to right: F. Wilson, G. Macdonald, L. Surman, T. Ballinger, H. Gilder.

GOTHERINGTON FOOTBALL TEAM photographed in 1930 in Cheltenham before a match. Back row, left to right: Claud Hobbs, Gorden Pullen, Chris Price, Lionel Watkins, Nobby Clark, Len Le Febve. Front row, left to right: Arthur Thompson, Harry Parker, Ernest Aston, Fred Upton, Jim Rendell.

BISHOP'S CLEEVE SECOND TEAM, 1934–35.

THE WINCHCOMBE 'BUFFALOES' in full regalia taken at Stanway House some time in the 1930s.

THE REST OF THIS SECTION contains a variety of different groups. To Winchcombe people these two photographs will probably bring the greatest pleasure. The enormous influence of Postlip Paper Mill on the town during most of the period being studied, is well illustrated by this cheerful print of the Adlards and their workforce taken in 1956 to mark the retirement of Albert Ballinger (standing in the centre front).

THERE IS A PHOTOGRAPH later in this volume of Winchcombe Hospital. This group consists of the staff and governors of the hospital taken in 1928, shortly after the hospital opened. Unfortunately the names of the nurses are not known, but the rest are, from left to right: Mrs Spiers, Major Dent-Brocklehurst, Miss Adlard, Mrs Cox, Mr Shipway, Miss Lewis (matron), Dr Robinson, Dr Murray, Dr Howell (in front), Dr Cox (behind), Dr Pim, Dr Soden.

CELEBRATIONS AT BANGROVE, between Teddington and Alstone. This group of over 40 years ago seem to have been celebrating Mr Sexty's eightieth birthday.

JUNE OLDACRE, Catherine Oldacre, Ellen Long and Hilda Oldacre in front of hayricks at Pecked Piece Farm, Bishop's Cleeve, in 1936.

STILL IN BISHOP'S CLEEVE – a Christmas party for the old folks held in the WI Hall in the early 1950s.

IN THE AREA many village pubs have undergone dramatic change in the last decade. The King's Head in Bishop's Cleeve remains relatively unaffected. Harry Clarke, Bill Leech and Herbert Washbourne pose for the camera with landlord Les Winters.

THE ELM TREE is no longer a pub. Just before the last war a group of its regulars stand in front of the landlord, Dick Chandler.

THIS MERRY GROUP was photographed at The Plough, Prestbury, c. 1950. Around landlady Kate Drew, readers might recognise Pat Bingham, Jack Boulton, John Roberts, George Pockett, George Excell, Tommy Ashley and Jack Morley.

SWITCHING FROM PRESTBURY TO WOOLSTONE, here are two more photographs taken at the Rectory fêtes before the last war. This group was taken in the same year as the scenes shown on page 59.

THE WAR BROUGHT AN END TO THE FÊTES. These young ladies (and two boys) were photographed in what was probably the last fête of all.

REFERENCE HAS ALREADY BEEN MADE in this section to the contribution made by Sunday Schools to education. They also provided opportunities for recreation. Woodmancote Chapel Sunday School pause before setting off for their annual outing in 1946.

ANOTHER COMMUNITY ACTIVITY in Woodmancote. The 'Skylarks' concert group conclude a performance at the old village hall in 1945.

WOODMANCOTE YOUTH CLUB thinly disguised as a cricket team, c. 1950.

WINNERS AT WOODMANCOTE FLOWER SHOW in 1935.

WE RETURN TO THE FIRST WINCHCOMBE CARNIVAL as we end this section. This card was sent by Gilbert (one of the pierrots) who complained that it was not a good picture of himself. Which one is Gilbert?

First
Winchcombe
Carnival

IT WOULD ALSO BE INTERESTING TO KNOW the identity of this mangificently dressed character.

93

THIS SECTION ENDS as it started with a typical portrait. In 1957 Arthur Lane was awarded a silver medal at the Three Counties' Show for over 50 years' work at Grange Farm, Woolstone. He left school at the age of ten to earn 3*d*. a day. Keeping him at school cost 2*d*. a week.

SECTION FOUR

Just Buildings

THE TWO PHOTOGRAPHS used to introduce this section illustrate some of the strengths and weaknesses of photographs of buildings in helping us build a picture of the past. This house at Didbrook is valuable for the historian as an example of a cruck frame. The early twentieth-century postcard tells us less than we could discover from visiting the spot today.

HOWEVER ... this photograph of Chamber's Cottage, Stanway, taken c. 1860 is far more valuable, because the house itself was demolished before the end of the last century.

HERE ARE TWO MORE CALOTYPES from Lord Neidpath's collection. This one provides a record of Stanway House before alteration in 1859. The ninth Earl of Wemyss and his wife succeeded in keeping still for the long exposure!

YET THIS PICTURE, taken about the same time, records little that is not the same today.

NOT FAR FROM STANWAY HOUSE lies the remains of Hailes Abbey – an increasingly popular tourist attraction. This sequence of photographs reminds us how much work has been put into their conservation. Note the high ground level in this view c. 1860.

Hayles Abbey, Gloucestershire.
The Cloister Arches.

SOME CLEARANCE had already been carried out by the time of these next two photographs taken 70 years later.

ANOTHER VIEW OF THE ARCHES.

THIS PROVIDES AN INTERESTING CONTRAST with today's museum. The glass-cased monks still remain.

ANOTHER LOCAL BUILDING photographed as a calotype is Sudeley Castle, seen here c. 1860.

COMPARE THIS with the previous photographs of Hailes. Here the neglect has increased in the 50 years between these two pictures.

THE CREEPERS ADD TO THE ROMANTIC EFFECT created on this Tovey postcard, posted in March 1907, bearing the message of what a lovely place this is.

AN OBVIOUSLY MORE MODERN, AERIAL VIEW on this postcard showing the grounds before the building of the car park.

NOT FAR FROM STANWAY HOUSE lies Toddington Manor, former home of Lord Sudeley. It was one of the last stately homes in the country to be built, between 1820 and 1835. This postcard shows its good condition in the early years of this century compared with today.

THERE ARE MANY OTHER LARGE HOUSES in the area under study. This is a photograph of Postlip House showing the Adlard family and servants (discreetly in the background) taken shortly after the house was built in 1886.

THE BILLIARD ROOM AT POSTLIP HOUSE laid out with wedding presents in 1910.

THE GREAT HOUSE IN BISHOP'S CLEEVE was the rectory. This print complements the one in the earlier volume. Both were taken c. 1890. Rector Hemming's daughter stands by the porch.

THE ORIGINAL RECTORY AT WOOLSTONE was first recorded in 1704. The left-hand part in this photograph of 1885 was added in the 1830s, but the whole building was devastated by fire in 1889. It took three hours for the fire brigade to arrive from Cheltenham.

THE RECTORY HAD BEEN REBUILT by 1897, but the rectors have never lived there. The photographs of Woolstone fêtes shown earlier in this were taken in the garden of the later rectory, opposite the church. This, too, is now a private house.

The Parish Church, Bishop's Cleeve.

STAYING WITH CHURCH BUILDINGS, Bishop's Cleeve parish church has not changed but fashions have, and most of the gravestones have been removed since this turn of the century postcard.

THE INTERIOR HAS CHANGED LITTLE, ALSO. Note, however, the oil lamps on this card posted in June 1925.

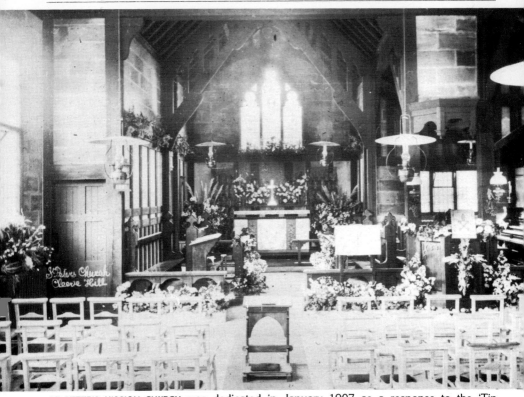

ST PETER'S MISSION CHURCH was dedicated in January 1907 as a response to the 'Tin Tabernacle' shown on page 19. This postcard was sent for Christmas 1910, and presumably shows the harvest festival earlier in that year.

AN EARLY TWENTIETH CENTURY VIEW of Alderton church. It shows how the surroundings of the church have changed even if the building looks the same.

ANOTHER PHOTOGRAPH to complement one in the earlier volume. Winchcombe Church before the 1872 restoration, showing the box pews and extraordinary flue for the heating stove.

THE CHURCH AT SOUTHAM forms part of a manorial complex with the Tithe Barn and Pigeon House. These two photographs show the latter in 1924 before the 'restoration' which deliberately made the buildings look 'old'.

IT IS WORTH A VISIT TO SOUTHAM just to see how successful the transformation was! This shows the side of the house facing away from the courtyard.

THE CORNER CUPBOARD has changed little during this century.

THE SHUTTER has changed a little since this photograph was taken 50 years ago. Note the gates at the side which led to cottages where the car park now extends.

THIS IS THE PHOTOGRAPH OF WINCHCOMBE HOSPITAL, referred to on page 85 in the previous section, and taken at the time of its opening in 1927.

COMPARING THIS SCENE with that on page 123 of *Bishop's Cleeve to Winchcombe in Old Photographs*, 20 years after opening in a disused quarry on Cleeve Hill in 1893, the site has matured. The Convalescent home was one of many taken over by the military during the First World War.

IT HAS BEEN VERY DIFFICULT TO FIND OLD PHOTOGRAPHS of farms and farm buildings. However, here is a valuable sequence showing Pecked Piece Farm which stood at the top of Pecked Lane in Bishop's Cleeve. Houses now cover the site. Linda Field stands in front of the farmhouse in February 1954.

THE YARD with its fascinating thatched buildings. A view taken in 1932.

TWENTY-TWO YEARS LATER little had changed on this farm.

HOWEVER, by the 1920s, Old Farm in Station Road had begun to offer coffee, lunch and tea.

GRETTON HILL FARM continues as a working farm under the Pullens today. This aerial photograph of 30 years ago shows traditional hayricks.

LANE END, GRETTON

THE LANE IS KNOWN AS DUGLINCH LANE; the cottage is now known as Orchard Cottage. The date of this picture is c. 1920.

ANOTHER GRETTON COTTAGE, now known as Shepherd's Cottage in Greenway Lane.

A COTTAGE ON THE TODDINGTON ESTATE, c. 1910. Since the Sudeleys left Toddington Manor the village has lost the atmosphere of an estate village which is still so obvious at neighbouring Stanway.

COTTAGES IN SOUTHAM LANE in the 1930s. A view looking the other way appeared in *Bishop's Cleeve to Winchcombe in Old Photographs* on page 156.

NOT AN INHABITED BUILDING, OF COURSE, but Winchcombe gasholder conveniently leads us into the next section 'Earning a Living', where we can learn more about this important part of Winchcombe's recent past.

THE NEXT SECTION STARTS HERE here with a reminder of the agricultural base of the area's economy until the last war. The first five photographs show Bert Long's farm at Pecked Piece in Bishop's Cleeve. They provide a fascinating picture of Bishop's Cleeve before its great expansion, and special thanks go to my long standing friend Derrick Blake, and Bert's daughter, Ellen, for making them available. Here Bert Long is seen milking 'in the field' off Stoke Road c. 1930.

Earning A Living

NEARER TO PECKED PIECE FARM. Bert drives the cows in for milking at about the same date as the previous picture.

MILKING ON THE FARM THIS TIME.

A SCENE that has just disappeared in recent years. Nell Long feeding the chickens.

THE LONG FAMILY – Ellen, Bert and Nell. A photograph taken in 1932.

BISHOP'S CLEEVE DAIRY has been the major supplier of milk to homes in Bishop's Cleeve and area since 1936. A view of the business taken c. 1948.

AN EARLIER MILK SCENE. Gretton Hill farm in 1922 with Charlie Busson and Prince about to take the milk to Greet Mill Dairy.

CLEEVE COMMON has played an important part in the economy of the area. John Denley (shepherd) and 'Pikey' Gaskins (stonemason) take their lunch by the Washpool in 1910.

TWENTY YEARS ON — sheep coming up from the Washpool under the watchful eye of haywarden Walter Denley (extreme left).

ANOTHER PRINT from Henry Branch's 1904 book *Cotswold and Vale*. It is entitled 'A Mowing Scene, Prestbury Park' and predates the present racecourse. As on the previous page, note the cider flagon.

AGAIN, NOTE THE CIDER FLAGON. This photograph reminds us of the threat to crops caused by the rabbit. A successful shoot from Yew Tree Farm, Gotherington, in the 1920s. Left to right: Edward Cook, Arthur Pullen, Reg Pitman, and Lewis Cook.

THESE PEOPLE picked the apples which made the cider. At Alderton c. 1912.

UNTIL THE LAST WAR, farming in the area was little mechanized. Horse and manure cart in the mud at Bengrove Farm 50 years ago.

A RARE EXAMPLE of a mechanical threshing machine, at work on Grange Farm, Woolstone, in 1956. It had been built in 1881 and was originally driven by steam. Note the number of men needed compared with a modern combine.

THE TRACTOR made an enormous difference in conditions like this. Earnest Lane ploughing with Woolstone's first tractor, bought in 1940, across 'Five Horses Land' – the name speaks for itself.

1949 PRODUCED A BUMPER POTATO HARVEST at Gretton Hill Farm. Maitland Pullen drives the tractor watched by William Martin while Mrs Robbins and Carol put the potatoes into the bucket.

MAITLAND AND MARGARET PULLEN bagging the crop.

POTATO PICKERS at a rather earlier date. Mr Sexty and helpers at Bengrove again.

ANOTHER PHOTOGRAPH of a 'first' tractor. Jack Minett in Bishop's Cleeve over 40 years ago.

THE VILLAGE SHOP continues to play an important part in the life of many villages. George Agg stands outside Alderton Post Office c. 1936.

SHOEMAKER CHARLES AGG poses proudly with his Ariel motor cycle and side-car in Alderton in 1925.

FRANK GOULD, proprietor of Northam Stores in Woodmancote for many years, photographed c. 1955. Many village shops started in house living rooms, as here.

MRS BECKINGSDALE and twins look out of the post office in 1910. It remained a traditional village shop until closure in 1984.

MR & MRS EDGINTON outside the bakery in Bishop's Cleeve before its demolition 25 years ago.

THE NOTICE BY THE DOOR READS 'Allen Duke, Surgeon, Frankfurt Lodge, Hewletts, attends at 12 o'clock Thursdays'. Various members of the Adcock family stand in front. The date, 1895; the place, Station Road, Bishop's Cleeve.

A FURTHER PHOTOGRAPH on a medical theme. Nurse Jenny Wolfe and daughter Mary with a donkey cart in Aggs Lane, Gotherington. Bert Staite holds the donkey.

AN IMMACULATE HORSE AND TRAP bringing the post from Winchcombe to Alderton around the turn of the century.

AN IMPORTANT INDUSTRY IN WINCHCOMBE has been the manufacture of gas since the 1850s. The original Winchcombe gasholder photographed in 1912. Ted Marsdon with his children, Archie and Edith.

THE DEMOLITION OF THE RETORT HOUSE. Ted and Archie Marsden with an unidentified helper, c. 1922.

THE LEISURE AND PLEASURE OF CHELTENHAM RACES FOR SOME, meant earning a living for others. More photographs from the Roberts' stable in Prestbury, both taken at the Hayes in the 1930s. Left to right: Tommy Cross, David Jones, Tommy Crabbe, Joe Bullock, John Roberts.

THIS PHOTOGRAPH MIGHT LACK ACTION, but not interest for local people: Joe Bullock, David Jones, Tommy Cross, Tommy Crabbe, John Roberts and Betty Roberts (now Betty Mustoe).

BEN ROBERTS, trainer; Jimmy Middleton, head lad; Bob Stone, horse; together in Albert Road, Pittville, when it still had the appearance of a country lane in 1930.

STABLE LADS at Morningside Cottage Stables. Right to left: 'Scat' Williams, Allan Richards, Joe Bullock, Tommy Crabbe, Jimmy Middleton.

TRADITIONAL CRAFTS do survive. Pete Pockett rethatching Randall's Cottage, Prestbury, in 1973.

On The Move

THROUGH THE GENEROSITY OF TIM PETCHEY, I have again been able to use some of the photographs held in his railway museum in Winchcombe. He has been able to name all the staff here at Winchcombe station in 1907 two years after opening: Mr Edwards (station-master), T. Phillips, F. Kemeys and J. Marshall (signalmen), B. Ashwin (porter), C. Eacock (checker), Mr Reynolds (clerk).

A MISHAP at Winchcombe on August Bank Holiday Saturday in 1939.

ANOTHER PERSON to whom I am indebted for railway photographs shown in this section is Bill Potter of Bishop's Cleeve. His sequence here shows the station on the last day of regular passenger services – 5 March 1960.

EVEN ON THE LAST DAY there were few people on the platform.

AFTER CLOSURE TO REGULAR TRAINS, Bishop's Cleeve station continued to be used occasionally on Race Days. Here the Royal Train leaves on Gold Cup day, 1963.

CHELTENHAM RACECOURSE had its own station. *Clun Castle* heads the last steam-hauled London special on the same day as the top photograph, 14 March 1963.

THE LAST OCCASION when the Racecourse station was used was recorded by Bill Potter. A diesel multiple unit came from Bristol for the Gold Cup in 1971.

OTHER PASSENGER TRAINS continued to use the line after the local trains ceased. It was sometimes used on summer Sundays for trains diverted from the Cheltenham–Birmingham mainline. This was the case on 18 June 1967, in a photograph showing another view of the Racecourse station.

UNTIL THE END OF SUMMER 1965, regular Wolverhampton–West Country Saturday expresses continued to use the line. *Grantley Hall* was photographed near Gretton on 25 July 1964.

THE BUG at Bishop's Cleeve in September 1965. It is easy to see how the twice-daily Gloucester–Leamington service gained its nickname.

TWO UNITS WERE JOINED TOGETHER when this photograph, looking across Prescott railway bridge, was taken on 26 February 1966.

A THREE-CAR UNIT was used on the last day of the operation of the service on 21 March 1968. It is seen here crossing Stanway viaduct near Toddington.

AFTER THE LOCAL PASSENGER SERVICE was withdrawn, goods traffic at Winchcombe continued until the end of 1964. This scene was taken shortly before that traffic ceased.

THE HONEYBOURNE LINE was used by trains carrying iron ore from the East Midlands to South Wales in the 1960s. One such train was photographed at Southam in July 1964.

THIS PHOTOGRAPH of an 'up' mixed goods train in July 1963 gives a general view of Bishop's Cleeve goods yard which had just been closed.

ANOTHER LINE, and not strictly in our area, but the Ashchurch–Birmingham line provided transport to Evesham and Birmingham for the villagers of Alderton. When this photograph of Beckford station was taken in April 1963 trains from Ashchurch ran only to Evesham because of the condition of the track beyond Evesham.

THIS SEQUENCE OF RAILWAY PHOTOGRAPHS ends with a contrast. All the previous photographs show lively scenes unrepeatable today. Compare here the dereliction at Toddington shortly before total closure in 1977, with the lively scene today created by the Gloucestershire and Warwickshire Railway, which has its headquarters at the station.

WE NOW TURN TO ROADS AND THEIR TRAFFIC, starting with a reminder of what Cotswold roads would be like before modern surfaces and drainage. Buckland, c. 1860.

INTERESTINGLY, THE ROAD TO NUTTERS-WOOD on Cleeve Hill still remains in a similar condition to that when it was photographed here c. 1900. The old lady has been to collect her gallon loaf of bread from the Rising Sun.

THE FIRST VOLUME OF OLD PHOTOGRAPHS included one of the Bishop's Cleeve fire engine at the Tithe Barn. Here is a second photograph of the machine in the capable care of Charles Trapp c. 1933.

A HORSE AND TRAP was the Victorian equivalent of the family car — for those who could afford it. Fanny Aldridge and Sarah Adcock are about to lead off with a trapful of relatives. Bishop's Cleeve c. 1895.

THESE TWO PHOTOGRAPHS mark the development of the modern road system compared with the two photographs on page 143, and yet provide an interesting contrast with today. Note the better surface, RAC phone box and County Council finger post on this postcard of Toddington, sent in May 1930.

THAT CROSSROADS WERE WORTHY OF BEING SUBJECTS FOR POSTCARDS tells us about the increasing importance of roads in the inter-war period. Careful observation will find a bus disappearing in the distance while a horse-drawn butcher's van stands outside the Cross Hands. Harry Evans was well-known as a local RAC man. Another scene c. 1930.

A PHOTOGRAPH, taken for the same postcard series as the previous photograph, of a house half a mile to the south of the crossroads. This was the age of the open road (for cyclists as well as motorists), with tea houses to cater for them.

WITHIN A COUPLE OF MILES OF 'CHEZ NOUS' stood another roadside café. Mrs Lord looked after it from c.1935 to the war years, which brought an end to this era of motoring. The café is still recognizable although it is now a private house.

THE GROWTH OF ROAD TRAFFIC brought with it problems of parking. Church Road, Bishop's Cleeve in 1958. On the left are the original roadside offices of Oldacres.

IT WAS UNDERSTANDABLE that such a large central open space as Abbey Terrace in Winchcombe should become a car park. This postcard dated August 1926 shows a car in the shadows and the 1887 water pump in the background. It links the other two postcards with the same view shown in the opening section of the book.

A FINAL REMINDER of the hazards that have faced all transport in this century. Another photograph of Station Road, Woodmancote, to add to those in my previous collection of old photographs. February 1947.

Echoes of a Wider World

NO STUDY OF A LOCAL AREA should end without some reference to the wider world. In *Bishop's Cleeve to Winchcombe in Old Photographs* I regretted the absence of any photograph of the prisoner-of-war camp at Sudeley. From Mrs M. Cato-Symonds of Staines in Middlesex came this photograph of the altar in the chapel, made by Italian prisoners-of-war from tin cans.

PRISONERS OF WAR worked on many local farms. At Bengrove Farm these Italians helped demolish an old barn.

AT GOTHERINGTON two Germans (kneeling behind the buckets) were photographed helping the Pullen family harvest potatoes near Cleeve Road.

THE IDENTITIES OF THESE SERVICEMEN remain unknown. They stand in the doorway to Sunnyside, No. 99 Gloucester Street, Winchcombe, and were presumably billetted in the area. Their message is, however, clear.

A WARTIME RIDE over Cleeve Hill, complete with gasmasks! Denzil Wolley leads, followed by Pat Symthe, Sylvia and Kathleen Malet. Note the once familiar but now vanished scene of a horse (on the skyline) grazing on the common.

THE WORST TRAGEDY IN THE AREA was probably the landing of a stray bomb in Shutter Lane, Gotherington in 1941. It destroyed the cottage of Elizabeth Kearsey who was killed, despite the rescue efforts organized by Revd C.D. Walker of Woolstone, which form the subject of this photograph.

BEFORE, DURING AND AFTER THE WAR Queen Mary was a regular visitor to Sudeley Castle. She is photographed here with the Dent-Brocklehurst family in 1949.

THE SOLE EXAMPLE in this volume from an earlier war – Winchcombe Special Constables during the First World War. The boy in the front is Jack Smith-Wood. The photogragh was taken in his back garden.

TO PEOPLE LIVING IN THE AREA, the most obvious change bringing them into close contact with the outside world in the early years of this century was the building of the railway. This is another of Tim Petchey's photographs showing the cutting west of the station in 1904.

THIS PANORAMA OF WINCHCOMBE STATION soon after opening in 1905 shows the impact of the railway on the community. Coal and other goods could be brought in easily; milk could be transported quickly; people could move in and out. In this photograph a Cheltenham Boys' Brigade company move off to camp, closely watched by station master Edwards from his garden.

ONE TIME when part, at least, of the area studied made itself heard to the wider world, occured when the popular wireless programme *Down Your Way* visited Bishop's Cleeve during the last war. Older readers might recognise Mr and Mrs S. Gilder, Mr C. Trapp, Mr W. Shipway, Mr F. Minett, Mr B. Haviland, Mrs M. Smith, Mrs F. Willetts and Mr J. Gass.

ACKNOWLEDGEMENTS

It is my pleasure to acknowledge the generous help given by the following people without whom this book could not have been compiled. They have not only lent photographs and given permission for them to be used, but have also given freely of their knowledge of the area. In several cases they are also owners of the copyright, which I also acknowledge here. I have made every effort to trace copyrights when they were known to exist.

G. Agg ● H. Archer ● B. Barton ● D. Blake ● P. Burchill ● M. Cato-Symonds
P. Christie ● D. Copson ● V . Counsell ● E. Coulson ● C. Cresswell
J. Crouch ● B. Cummings ● T. Curr ● H. Denham ● J. Doxsey ● V. Evans
A. Evason ● C. Fennell ● C. Footer ● V. Gardner ● E. Hopkins ● D. Hornby
M. Lashford Spinks ● E. Long ● K. Malet ● B. Mustoe ● Lord Neidpath
B. Nutbourne ● M. Page ● J. Petchey ● T. Petchey ● W. Potter ● M. Pullen
O. Pullen ● W. Pullen ● S. Sadler ● W. Sparks ● O. Stinchcombe ● D. Taylor
D. Tidmarsh ● W. Walker ● D. Waters ● J. Whitaker.

Additionally I wish to thank Judith Harvey at Alan Sutton Publishing for her patience and efficient administration. Finally, to my family, Margaret, Peter and Timothy, for their understanding and forbearance while I was compiling this volume, I give my greatest thanks. I alone, however, am responsible for any shortcomings in the work.

David H. Aldred
November 1989.